Boundless Love

A Women of Faith® Interactive and Application Guide

W PUBLISHING GROUP™

www.wpublishinggroup.com

A Division of Thomas Nelson, Inc.
www.ThomasNelson.com

Published by W Publishing Group, a Division of Thomas Nelson, Inc., P.O. Box 141000, Nashville, TN 37214.

Unless otherwise indicated, Scripture quotations used in this book are taken from the New King James Version (NKJV), copyright © 1979, 1980, 1982, 1992, Thomas Nelson, Inc. Used by permission. All rights reserved. Other quotations are taken from the following sources:

The King James Version of the Bible (KJV).

The Message (MSG) by Eugene Peterson. Copyright © 1993, 1994, 1995, 1996, 2000. Used by permission of NavPress Publishing Group. All rights reserved.

The Holy Bible, New International Version (NIV). Copyright © 1973, 1978, 1984 International Bible Society. Used by permission of Zondervan Bible Publishers. All rights reserved.

ISBN 0-8499-4379-5

Printed in the United States of America

02 03 04 05 06 — 9 8 7 6 5 4 3 2 1

Contents

His Love Never Ends

Give thanks to the LORD, for he is good; his love endures forever.
—1 CHRONICLES 16:34 (NIV)

The lights go down, the praise goes up, and the Women of Faith Boundless Love conference sweeps you into an uproarious celebration of the boundless, fearless, lavish, stubborn, outlandish, intentional love of God.

Warning: When you've completed this conference experience, you won't be the same woman you were when you started. Throughout these laughter-lined, tear-cleansed, heart-thrilling sessions led by speakers Sheila Walsh, Patsy Clairmont, Thelma Wells, Barbara Johnson, Marilyn Meberg, and Luci Swindoll, you'll come to know and personalize God's unfathomable love for you in a way you've probably never felt before. As these dynamic Christian speakers share lessons and insights focused on the boundless love of God, you'll feel yourself being renewed, restored, and readied to pass along the blessings of that love to others. In the time ahead, we hope the teaching of Ephesians 5:1 will become a way of life for you:

Watch what God does, and then you do it, like children who learn proper behavior from their parents. Mostly what God does is love you. Keep company with him and learn a life of love. Observe how Christ loved us. His love was not cautious, but extravagant. He didn't love in order to get something from us but to give everything of himself to us. Love like that. (MSG)

Getting the Most
from Your Boundless Love
Conference Experience

The Women of Faith Boundless Love conference features six outstanding speakers who offer their perspectives on the nature of God's boundless love and the profoundly personal effect it can have on the lives of women. This interactive and application guide has been designed to help you enjoy, remember, reflect on, and apply the wisdom and lessons shared by these six enthusiastic sisters in Christ.

We've organized the materials into a series of eight sessions, but of course you can use the videos and workbook any way you choose. You may enjoy using these materials on your own as a richly rewarding daily devotional. If so, you have the freedom to choose your own scheduling and timing preferences.

If you're sharing the Boundless Love conference experience with others, we've included two lesson-plan formats for each session to assist groups both large and small. Choose the format that works best for your allotted time and setting.

Promoting Your Gatherings

Showing the seventeen-minute Introduction and Welcoming Vignettes on Tape 1 is a great way to promote your upcoming Women of Faith Boundless Love conference experience. The zany introductory video and insightful (and funny) vignettes give potential participants an idea of the format and content of Boundless Love. It also encourages them to register and get the workbooks so they can participate.

Choosing a Group Format and Planning the Sessions

The *Boundless Love Women of Faith Interactive and Application Guide* offers two outlined formats for use with small or large groups. If you have ninety minutes or more to devote to each session, you can use the Full-Length Option. If you only have sixty minutes to spend per session, the Fast-Track Option will probably work best for you. The difference in the two options is that the Full-Length Option includes showing each speaker's two-minute Welcoming Vignette before her main presentation (or having a participant read aloud the vignette script); on the Fast-Track Option, you read the script before the session begins and then skip directly to the main presentation. The other difference in the two options is that the Full-Length Option allows time for discussing the Back-Stage Pass Bible Studies as a group. If you follow the shorter Fast-Track Option, you or your group members should use the Bible studies as a means of reviewing the topics between sessions.

Because these video presentations were originally taped during a weekend Women of Faith conference, they make an excellent series for a Friday-night/all-day-Saturday schedule, such as a women's retreat, a weekend church-women's conference, or similar gathering.

Managing Your Time

If you're using the videos and workbook in a group setting, we encourage you to stick to the proposed schedule as much as possible. Gently encourage the women to participate and express their thoughts but to keep their remarks brief. Don't let discussions wander off-topic. Group gatherings—especially gatherings of women who may have family, work, or schooling commitments—are most successful when participants can depend on every session beginning and ending on time. Each session outline includes a time line for both the Full-Length and Fast-Track Options suggesting the time to be allotted for each part of the session.

In case you're adapting the videos for your own customized schedule, the following list shows you the time required for the main video segment corresponding to each session. Remember that you may also choose to play each speaker's two-minute Welcoming Vignette during her session before continuing on to her main video presentation. The thought-provoking lesson plans for each of the sessions will guide you in using the rest of your allotted time to discuss and apply the speaker's message.

Session 1—Introduction and Welcoming Vignettes (17 minutes)

Session 2—Sheila Walsh (35 minutes)

Session 3—Patsy Clairmont (35 minutes)

Session 4—Thelma Wells (35 minutes)

Session 5—Barbara Johnson (12 minutes)

Session 6—Marilyn Meberg (44 minutes)

Session 7—Luci Swindoll (40 minutes)

Session 8—Sheila Walsh (15 minutes)

Using the Workbook and Videos

No matter whether you follow the Full-Length or the Fast-Track Option or choose to develop your own time line, each session is designed to reveal to you the rich, rewarding blessings of God's boundless love. While the Introductory and Wrap-Up Sessions are less structured, the six main sessions, on both the Full-Length and Fast-Track Options, are divided into the following seven segments plus notes to the group leader:

Leader's Notes. These self-explanatory notes are included throughout the workbook for group leaders who are facilitating discussions during the sessions. Participants in groups can also review these guidelines to gain a sense of where the facilitator might direct the discussion. These notes, however, are merely suggestions.

Introductions, Greetings, and Prayer. Women of Faith conferences are well known for the camaraderie they create. We've intentionally left this part of the session outline unscripted so that your gathering can begin as a warm, informal gathering of friends. The leader should introduce herself and then ask participants to reintroduce themselves at the beginning of each session. For variety, or as an "icebreaker," ask each woman to say her name and tell one new thing about herself ("I have six children" or "I grew up in Alaska" or "I collect old Bibles"). If the group is auditorium-sized, ask each woman to do the same with the four women to her right and left and in front and back of her (always reminding everyone to be brief—this is an introduction time, not a discussion session!). Note that this segment is allotted five minutes in the Full-Length Option, three minutes in the Fast-Track Option.

The leader should then briefly summarize that you're following the *Boundless Love Women of Faith Interactive and Application Guide,* reminding the women that last week you heard _____ speaking on _____, and during this session you'll be listening to and discussing _____'s presentation on _____ . For example, the leader might say, "Last week we enjoyed Sheila's presentation on Boundless Love. This morning we'll be hearing and discussing Patsy's perspective on Fearless Love."

Setting the Stage.

At the beginning of the Women of Faith conference, each speaker presents a two-minute Welcoming Vignette that evokes laughter and delivers memorable insights. These vignettes are so revealing of each speaker's lifestyle and personality that we include the vignette scripts here at the beginning of each speaker's workbook session. If you've chosen the Full-Length Option, we suggest you replay each speaker's Welcoming Vignette from Tape 1 during that session's Setting the Stage segment. If you're following the Fast-Track Option, you will skip the Welcoming Vignette videos, so you should read the vignette transcript in the Setting the Stage segment *before* the session so you can go directly to the Main Event. The exception to this time line is Barbara Johnson's presentation in Session 5. Because of the brevity of Barbara's main video presentation, you will have time to view the Welcoming Vignette video as well as the main presentation.

Main Event.

These speakers are on a mission—and they don't dillydally around as they're laying out their battle plans! This section of the workbook is designed to make notetaking simple. We suggest that you read through each session's Main Event section before viewing the videotape so you'll know what to listen for. Then, as you watch the presentation, you'll be prepared to fill in the blanks and keep track of the speaker's main points as she takes you through her perspective of God's boundless love.

Taking It to Heart.

There's a fine line between laughter and tears, and you'll find it often gets erased during these sessions. Part of the benefit of watching and listening to these women comes from the experience itself. They're good company! They're the kind of friends who lift your spirits by their very presence. Their words remind you that others share your experiences and thoughts as a woman and that, contrary to what you may sometimes feel, you really are not alone. It's encouraging to know that others have walked the same path and have lived to talk about it. You can benefit from their stories.

Be careful not to rush through the Taking It to Heart sections. These spaces and questions will allow you to record your feelings and thoughts while the session lessons are fresh in your mind. Consider the questions carefully and be honest in your answers.

If you are working through this study with a group, you will have a rich opportunity to add your own story to the encouragement offered by the conference speakers. If necessary, break the participants into small groups to briefly share your thoughts with each other, remembering that you may find that someone in your group has just as much to teach you as the amazing women on the screen. God has a wonderful way of putting these people in front of us, one way or another!

Taking It Home.
Now comes the hard part—application. Women of Faith has a mission statement that begins,

> Women of Faith's mission is to see women set free to a lifestyle of God's truth and grace.

These women and the organization they represent hope to impact your life for the better. That's how the effectiveness of this experience will ultimately be measured: by the way it changes you. As you enjoy this conference experience, we hope your view of God and of yourself, your attitude toward the world around you, and the way you live become more Christlike, more reflective of God's boundless love. Use the questions in the Taking It Home section to apply the lessons in the session to yourself and to work out your life plan in the context of God's boundless love.

Back-Stage Pass—Bible Studies.
Each of the six speakers has spoken from the things hidden in her heart combined with lessons from God's Word. Behind each story and idea these women share, you will find a deep desire to communicate the truth from Scripture.

This section offers Bible studies that take you into the passages to which the speakers referred, along with other relevant statements from Scripture. The material is designed to help you learn the lessons they shared as well as hide them in your heart. Depending on whether you're following the Full-Length or Fast-Track Option, you may complete these

Bible studies in your group or on your own as a means of reviewing between sessions. The exception to the time-line schedule again comes in Session 5. Because of the brevity of Barbara Johnson's Main Event segment, you will have time to complete the Session 5 Back-Stage Pass segment as a group.

Everyone has her own preferred translation of the Bible, and we hope you'll bring yours to each session and use it to study the highlighted passages. In case it's more convenient for you, though, we've included most of the passages in the session plans. You may find that the Bible passages quoted by the speakers differ from those translations printed here or from your own favorite translation, but you will be able to follow their teaching without a problem. Many times it enhances a Bible study to observe how the different Bible versions translate a particular passage.

A Last Word—and Closing Prayer. Each session ends with a final thought to share before closing your Boundless Love experience with prayer. This section highlights at least one central, memorable insight from the speaker's session. Think about the closing thought presented here as an idea to ponder during the coming week.

Here We Go!

God has loved you from the beginning—from the beginning of your life, from the beginning of the world. No matter what you have or have not done, no matter how long you've strayed or how far you've fallen, he has never stopped loving you—and he never will. The Women of Faith Boundless Love conference doesn't change anything about God's love for you; it is time-less and eternal, and it has been there all along. But the journey you're about to begin just might change the way you think about that boundless, all-encompassing, never-ending love of God. And that could make an amazing difference in the way you live your life.

Are you ready for a life-changing experience? Turn the page, dim the lights, and cue up the video. The Women of Faith Boundless Love conference experience is about to begin!

Introduction

Sharing a Laughter-Filled Life: Ooey-Gooey Love Stories, Tattoos, Tangled Kite Strings, and Grandma-Style Goofiness

Leader's
NOTES

This session is intentionally unscripted so that the members of your group can spend informal time getting acquainted.

Open the session with a warm welcome, then lead the group in prayer, asking God to prepare your hearts and minds for the journey you're undertaking. Next ask someone to read aloud the verse from Ephesians 5 at the end of "His Love Never Ends" on page v. Finally, view the seventeen-minute Introduction and Welcoming Vignettes segment at the beginning of Tape 1. Stop the tape after Luci's vignette.

Use the remainder of the time to get to know each other. Go around the room or the table (or divide an auditorium-sized gathering into small groups of four to six women), inviting each participant to introduce herself and share one fact about herself she would like the others to know (for example, where she lives or works, her favorite hobby, or the title of the last book she read). When the hubbub has quieted, invite the participants to share other brief glimpses into their lives, suggesting one or more of the following get-acquainted topics:

1. Invite the women to briefly talk about why they have chosen to participate in this conference experience and what needs they hope it will fill in their lives.

2. Ask them to express what God's boundless love means to them now, as the series begins. We'll ask this question again later, in the Wrap-Up Session at the end.

3. Use the speakers' Welcoming Vignettes as a springboard for other discussion. Ask the women to say which one of the speakers' Welcoming Vignettes applied most personally to her. Notice who's wearing the "clunky, black, old grandma shoes" and who has on comfy Reeboks. Does anyone have a tattoo she wants to show? Does anyone else have plastic flowers planted in her front yard?

Preparing for Next Time. Read through Session 2 in the workbook before the next meeting, and don't forget to bring your Bible. If you're following the Fast-Track Option, it's especially important to read the script of Sheila's Welcoming Vignette in the Setting the Stage segment, as this video will not be shown during your session.

Boundless Love

SHEILA WALSH:

It's Time to Fly!

Full-Length Option (90 minutes)

Introductions (5 minutes)

Welcome

Opening Prayer

Setting the Stage (2 minutes to review Sheila's Welcoming Vignette on Tape 1)

Main Event (Tape 1—35 minutes)

Taking It to Heart (15 minutes)

Back-Stage Pass—Bible Studies (15 minutes)

A Last Word and Closing Prayer (3 minutes)

Fast-Track Option (60 minutes)

Introductions (3 minutes)

Brief Welcome and Opening Prayer

Setting the Stage (Read the Welcoming Vignette script on your own before the session begins.)

Main Event (Tape 1—35 minutes)

Taking It to Heart (10 minutes)

Taking It Home (10 minutes)

Back-Stage Pass—Bible Studies (Complete these Bible studies later at your convenience.)

A Last Word and Closing Prayer (3 minutes)

Setting the Stage

Leader's NOTES

If you're following the Fast-Track Option, skip now to the Main Event. If you're following the Full-Length Option, have Tape 1 cued to Sheila's Welcoming Vignette and play it now, during the Setting the Stage segment. At the end of the vignette, fast-forward the tape so it's ready to play Sheila's main presentation. Or, if this fast-forwarding procedure is awkward for you, cue the tape to Sheila's main presentation and ask a member of the group to read aloud the script *Tied in Knots* now.

Through the two-minute Welcoming Vignettes, each of the Women of Faith speakers introduces herself with a revealing glimpse into her style, thinking, and sense of humor. Sheila Walsh's Welcoming Vignette shares an illustration from her favorite source—her son.

Sheila's Welcoming Vignette: Tied in Knots

One day my son, Christian, and I were out in the yard, flying his kite. It was a wonderful day with a strong wind. I stopped and went inside to get us something to drink. He came running in after me and said, "Mommy, Mommy, please, you need to come back and help. There's a bird with his leg caught in the string of my kite!"

I went outside and, sure enough, there was a tiny, little bird all caught up in the string of Christian's kite.

He said, "Mommy, could we please help the bird?"

So I gently picked the bird up. It pecked my hand, it was so afraid. I managed to unwind all the string . . . and set it free.

Later that evening, my husband, Barry, and Christian and I were having our evening walk. A little bird flew overhead, singing its little song. Christian stopped and said (looking up), "You're welcome!"

Maybe you relate to that little bird. Maybe you've come here this weekend and you feel as if you're tied in knots inside. But if anyone ever even tried to help you, to get close enough to reach out and hold you, you would fight them. Do you know what the wonderful news is? Every one of us has been there. But Jesus Christ is here this weekend. He will take you in the center of his hand and gently untie all the string. And he'll say to you and say to me, "Fly!"

Main Event

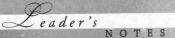 *Leader's* NOTES

When you preview the video, fill out this section yourself so you can anticipate some of the responses to Sheila's message. This preparation will also give you an idea of how much time you should allow at the end of the video for people to finish making notes. Remember to have your group take a moment to preview the Main Event section before viewing the video so everyone's ready to fill in the blanks and jot down notes during the video showing.

Video Presentation by Sheila Walsh: The Birdcage

One Sunday morning a pastor brought an unusual item to his pulpit. He came up and stood in front of the lectern with this in his hand [a birdcage]. He told this story:

A few days ago a man was walking down a country lane and came across a young boy carrying this birdcage. The man said, "What do you have there, son?"

The boy said, "Oh, it's just an old birdcage and I have a couple of old birds in it."

The man looked in, and there they were in the bottom of the cage, shivering, frightened. He asked, "What are you going to do with those birds?"

"Oh, I don't know," the boy said. "I'll poke a stick at them . . . torment them a bit. You know, if you pull their feathers out, you can make them fight with one another."

The man asked, "Then what are you going to do?"

The boy said, "Well, then I'm going to kill them."

"How much do you want for those birds?" the man asked.

The boy said, "You don't want them. They don't sing . . . they're not very pretty. If you try to help them, they'll peck your hand."

The man asked again, "How much do you want for them?"

The boy looked at the man, summed him up, and said, "Ten dollars!"

"Done." The man gave the boy the money and took the cage. He set it down on the country lane and opened the door. Tapping gently on the bars, he said, "Come on, fly."

One day Satan came into the presence of Jesus. Satan had just come from the Garden of Eden. He said, "Look what I've got. I've got them all."

Jesus said, "What are you going to do with them?"

Satan answered, "I'll make them fight a little bit. You know, I can even make them hate one another and kill one another."

Jesus said, "Then what are you going to do?"

Satan said, "Oh, I'll kill them."

Jesus asked, "How much do you want for them?"

Satan answered, "All your tears, and all your blood."

And Jesus said, "Done."

Then he took the birdcage, set it down, opened the door, tapped gently on the bars, and said, "Come on, fly!"

The Bible lesson Sheila illustrates with her birdcage story is . . .

_____

_____

_____

Give three possible explanations for why we don't fly. (Sheila covers these twice. Finish the sentence and then add notes where needed.)

1. We're waiting until _____.

_____

_____

Let me just say from my own experience everything—every single thing I've ever put on a list of "If I just had this, if I just had that"— when I've gotten those things, they don't fit. Everything apart from Christ himself is a poor substitute, an imposter. (Sheila)

What does not satisfy when we find it is not what we were actually desiring.

—C. S. Lewis

2. We're not sure _____

_____

_____

_____

During her second review of the number 2 reason we don't fly, Sheila refers to a book by Karl Olsson called *Come to the Party!* The following points outline her comments.

- Karl Olsson describes the two kinds of believers that he meets as . . .

  The blessed: those who _____

  _____

  The unblessed: those who _____

  _____

- Sheila often tells her son, Christian, when she tucks him into bed, "If there were forty million four-year-old boys in the world and God said, 'You can be the mommy to any one of them,' _____

  _____."

- Sheila talks about the way Olsson describes four groups who have been invited to the party by Christ. The blank lines are for your notes about these groups. Group A. We don't believe there's a party. _____

  _____

  _____

  _____

I used to fall into group A. I used to have this desperately intense, serious calling on my life that made me think that I had to prove to God how much I love him, by being miserable down here, doing everything I think I would hate. I decided I'd be a missionary to India (as if India didn't have enough problems!). I decided that I would go because I couldn't think of anything I would hate more. I don't like traveling. I don't like creepy crawlies, but I thought, "Surely that will show you, God, that I love you because I'm not going to party. I'll have a deep joy, deep, deep, deep. But there is no joy, no party." (Sheila)

Group B. We believe there's a party but don't really believe we're invited.

_____

_____

Our circumstances do not determine our future— Jesus Christ does.

—Sheila

Group C. We believe there's a party, and we go, but we leave before anyone notices we're there.

_____

_____

_____

_____

Group D. We go to the party, and we stay! _____

_____

_____

_____

Notes on Sheila's comments about 2 Corinthians 4 and "cardboard boxes." (Also see the Bible study on this passage later in the session.)

_____

_____

_____

_____

3. The third reason we don't fly: We're too_____.

_____

_____

I spent so much of my time trying, like the cowardly lion, to find courage. I thought I just needed to become more courageous. No, anytime I think it goes back to me, I'm in trouble. Anytime I get back to thinking this is what I need to do . . . wrong! It's all about God. So I realized . . . Sheila, you'll always be a bit of a wuss, but what you need to do is to fix your eyes on him. The more I learn about him, the more I can say yes. (Sheila)

> *Living fearlessly is not the absence of fear but the presence of God.*
>
> *—Sheila*

Taking It to Heart
Questions to help you personalize the lessons in the session

1. Sheila offered three explanations for why, even though Christ has opened the door of our birdcages, we don't fly. Which of these most closely describes your way of life?

_____ I can't fly until I'm ready.

_____ I don't really think I was meant to fly.

_____ I'm just too afraid to fly.

2. What reasons or experiences have created that kind of response to freedom in you?

_____

_____

3. If you could ask Sheila one or two questions about what she talked about, what would they be? _____

_____

4. What parts of Sheila's comments did you find most helpful, and why?

_____

_____

Taking It Home

Questions to help you apply the lessons in the session

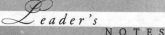

Leader's NOTES

Sheila's presentation has touched on the full range of emotions. Her stories may have opened wounds, revived dormant memories, and brought both laughter and tears. The most difficult part of your role is to know when to stick with the script and when to respond to the group's responses. By the time you get to this point in the session, the group may have discovered its own pace and needs. It's probably more important in the long run that the women get their needs heard and responded to than that the lesson be completely "filled out." However, keep in mind Sheila's central point—ultimately it's not about us and our needs; it's about God. No matter how far the group strays, bring them back to that point.

1. Sheila talked about containers—birdcages and cardboard boxes. She talked about little birds and eagles. How do these illustrations represent the life you really want to live?

_____

_____

_____

_____

2. Sheila admits, "Anytime I think it goes back to me, I'm in trouble. Anytime I get back to thinking this is what I need to do . . . wrong! It's all about God." In what ways do you think that attitude change would significantly affect your life?

_____

_____

_____

_____

3. What kinds of statements and requests would you like to present to God as this "flying" adventure begins? In what ways do you want him to make you more truly a woman of faith?

_____

_____

_____

_____

Back-Stage Pass—Bible Studies

Scripture passages used by Sheila Walsh

It is important to keep in mind that all the Women of Faith speakers are committed to basing their teaching on the Bible. Underlying their honesty and vulnerability is their genuine desire to communicate timeless truth from the Word of God.

If you're following the Fast-Track Option and using the Back-Stage Pass segment as a means of reviewing between meetings, direct the women now to skip to A Last Word at the end of the session and complete the Bible studies later, at their convenience. If your group is following the Full-Length Option, you will have fifteen minutes to work together through the following discussion of Sheila's selected Bible passages in this session. Ask one of the participants to read each passage aloud, then guide the women through the questions that follow. If time runs out, you may have to complete the Bible studies later at home. You'll have an opportunity during the Wrap-Up Session to share some of the insights you note here.

Psalm 63 (NIV)
A psalm of David. When he was in the Desert of Judah.

O God, you are my God,
    earnestly I seek you;
my soul thirsts for you,
    my body longs for you,
in a dry and weary land
    where there is no water.

²I have seen you in the sanctuary
    and beheld your power and your glory.
³Because your love is better than life,
    my lips will glorify you.
⁴I will praise you as long as I live,
    and in your name I will lift up my hands.
⁵My soul will be satisfied as with the richest of foods;
    with singing lips my mouth will praise you.

⁶On my bed I remember you;

    I think of you through the watches of the night.

⁷Because you are my help,

    I sing in the shadow of your wings.

⁸My soul clings to you;

    your right hand upholds me.

⁹They who seek my life will be destroyed;

    they will go down to the depths of the earth.

¹⁰They will be given over to the sword

    and become food for jackals.

¹¹But the king will rejoice in God;

    all who swear by God's name will praise him,

    while the mouths of liars will be silenced.

Psalm 63 Study Questions

1. In the first five verses, how does David use his circumstances as a way to think about his relationship with God?

_____

_____

2. When Sheila used the beautiful phrase from verse 3—"your love is better than life"—to talk about her relationship with God, what do you think she meant?

_____

_____

3. What would you mean if you said to God, in the psalmist's words, "your love is better than life"?

_____

_____

_____

Sheila talks about the things that we think are conditions for happiness or our readiness to fly (husband, child, health, etc.). Then she points to her own experience: "Everything—every single thing I've ever put on a list of 'If I just had this, if I just had that'—when I've gotten those things, they don't fit. Everything apart from Christ himself is a poor substitute, an imposter."

4. How do we keep the desires and concerns of life from coming between ourselves and God?

_____

_____

5. How does this psalm give us glimpses into the life of someone whose attitude consistently placed God in the center of his life?

_____

_____

6. What are some specific concerns, persons, sins, habits, or values that you realize occupy the center of your life more than God? What will it take to displace them?

_____

_____

Take a moment to put the thoughts and struggles you just listed in question 6 into the form of a prayer. Tell God how you desire to recognize him as the only one worthy to occupy the center of your life. _____

_____

_____

2 Corinthians 4:1–18

Therefore, since we have this ministry, as we have received mercy, we do not lose heart. [2]But we have renounced the hidden things of shame, not walking in craftiness nor handling the word of God deceitfully, but by manifestation of the truth commending ourselves to every man's conscience in the sight of God. [3]But even if our gospel is veiled, it is veiled to those who are perishing, [4]whose minds the god of this age has blinded, who do not believe, lest the light of the gospel of the glory of Christ, who is the image of God, should shine on them. [5]For we do not preach ourselves, but Christ Jesus the Lord, and ourselves your bondservants for Jesus' sake. [6]For it is the God who commanded light to shine out of darkness, who has shone in our hearts to give the light of the knowledge of the glory of God in the face of Jesus Christ.

[7]But we have this treasure in earthen vessels, that the excellence of the power may be of God and not of us. [8]We are hard pressed on every side, yet not crushed; we are perplexed, but not in despair; [9]persecuted, but not forsaken; struck down, but not destroyed—[10]always carrying about in the body the dying of the Lord Jesus, that the life of Jesus also may be manifested in our body. [11]For we who live are always delivered to death for Jesus' sake, that the life of Jesus also may be manifested in our mortal flesh. [12]So then death is working in us, but life in you.

[13]And since we have the same spirit of faith, according to what is written, "I believed and therefore I spoke," we also believe and therefore speak, [14]knowing that He who raised up the Lord Jesus will also raise us up with Jesus, and will present us with you. [15]For all things are for your sakes, that grace, having spread through the many, may cause thanksgiving to abound to the glory of God.

[16]Therefore we do not lose heart. Even though our outward man is perishing, yet the inward man is being renewed day by day. [17]For our light affliction, which is but for a moment, is working for us a far more exceeding and eternal weight of glory, [18]while we do not look at the things which are seen, but at the things which are not seen. For the things which are seen are temporary, but the things which are not seen are eternal.

2 Corinthians 4:1–18 Study Questions

An introductory thought from Sheila:

Now, to say to the people in Corinth that we have this treasure in earthenware pots is like saying to us tonight, here, that we have this treasure in cardboard boxes. That's what earthenware pots were in Corinth—the most common thing you stored things in. There is nothing special about earthenware pots. It's kind of arrogant, really, our thinking that we have to be ready to serve God. How ready does a cardboard box have to be? It just has to be there. And that's why, when you look around, you think that some of these people should be here, but not you. You think, "But look at them and look at me."

When Barry and I were making our last move, I called a company to ask about boxes for shipping. The man asked me, "Do you want new or used boxes?"

I asked him, "What's the difference?"

He said, "Nothing really. The used boxes are fine; they might have some tape on them, but they're cheaper."

Being Scottish by nature, as my sister can tell you, I said, "I'll take the used boxes, thank you very much." The boxes were not the point. It didn't matter if they had tape and writing on them as long as they held what was inside. So you can look around and say, "Oh, they look like new boxes, and I look like a tattered old box." Doesn't matter. The box is not the point; the point is the treasure inside the box. We are cardboard boxes to contain this treasure.

1. Both verses 1 and 16 repeat a central thought on Paul's mind—an identical phrase of five words: We do not _____

2. In verses 2–15, Paul offers at least five reasons that keep him from losing heart. What are they?

    a. Verse 2 _____

    _____

    b. Verses 3–4 _____

    _____

    c. Verses 5–6 _____

    d. Verse 7 _____

    _____

    e. Verses 8–15 _____

    _____

3. What other examples or illustrations of Sheila's "cardboard boxes" can you find in these verses?

    _____

    _____

4. What things make it difficult for you to center your attention on God and depend daily on him?_____

_____

_____

5. Based on Sheila's perspective, what thought do you want to remember the next time you feel discouraged and are tempted to "lose heart"?

_____

_____

_____

A Last Word

An insight from this session to remember until next time

Closing Thought: A witty Englishman named G. K. Chesterton is reported to have once remarked, "The real reason angels can fly is because they take themselves so lightly." Sheila has set the stage for the lessons to come by gently encouraging us to think a little more lightly of ourselves so that we might be able to appreciate and see God more clearly. She ends with an uplifting thought:

Even though eagles are some of the most magnificent, strongest birds in the world, they don't fly well on their own. They build their nests high in the mountains so that when the wind comes underneath them, they spread their wings and are carried aloft. So it is for us. Are you waiting to feel ready? This is as ready as we get. Not sure you were meant to fly? You were *made* to fly. Too afraid? Spend more time with the Father. It's not about us. It's about him.

Fearless Love

PATSY CLAIRMONT:

What Weapon Do You Reach for When Fear Comes Barking?

Full-Length Option (90 minutes)

Introductions (5 minutes)

Welcome

Opening Prayer

Setting the Stage (2 minutes to play Patsy's Welcoming Vignette on Tape 1—or to have someone read the vignette script aloud)

Main Event (Tape 1—35 minutes)

Taking It to Heart (15 minutes)

Taking It Home (15 minutes)

Back-Stage Pass—Bible Studies (15 minutes)

A Last Word and Closing Prayer (3 minutes)

Fast-Track Option (60 minutes)

Introductions (3 minutes)

Brief Welcome and Opening Prayer

Setting the Stage (Read the Welcoming Vignette script on your own before the session begins.)

Main Event (Tape 1—35 minutes)

Taking It to Heart (10 minutes)

Taking It Home (10 minutes)

Back-Stage Pass—Bible Studies (Complete these Bible studies later at your convenience.)

A Last Word and Closing Prayer (3 minutes)

Setting the Stage

𝓛eader's NOTES

If you're following the Fast-Track Option, skip now to the Main Event. If you're following the Full-Length Option and it's too awkward for you to play Patsy's two-minute Welcoming Vignette on Tape 1 and then fast-forward to find her main presentation, just cue the tape to the main presentation and ask someone to read aloud the vignette script, below.

Patsy Clairmont introduces herself with an illustration about the unexpected delights of aging. As you watch (or read), think about your own expectations and fears about life down the road.

Patsy's Welcoming Vignette: Those Grandma Shoes

I love being a grandmother. But I was a little concerned just before I became one, for one reason, and someone put it into poem form. Maybe this has crossed your mind as well:

> When I was very little, all the grandmas that I knew
> Used to walk around this world in ugly grandma shoes.
> You know the ones I speak of, those clunky-heeled kind,
> They just looked so very awful that it weighed upon my mind!
> For I knew when I grew old I'd have to wear those shoes,
> I'd think of that from time to time; it seemed like such bad news.
> But now when I go shopping what I see fills me with glee,
> For in my jeans and Reeboks I'm as comfy as can be,

And I look at all those teenage girls and there, upon their feet,

Are clunky, black, old grandma shoes,

And they think they're really neat!

Main Event

Leader's NOTES

When you preview the video, fill out this section yourself so you can anticipate some of the responses to Patsy's message. This preparation will also give you an idea of how much time you should allow at the end of the video for group members to finish making notes. Before viewing the video, remind the women to take a moment to preview the Main Event section so everyone's ready to fill in the blanks and jot down notes during the video showing.

Video Presentation by Patsy Clairmont:
How the Kirby Got in Bed with Me

On this evening in Michigan it was really, really cold. Our boys had already gone to sleep, two young sons at that time, and my husband and I nestled down into bed and fell sound asleep.

Several hours into the night, the phone rang. Don't you hate it when the phone rings late at night like that? You're afraid to pick it up. We did, though, and it was bad news, but nothing tragic. My parents lived in the next town, and their furnace had broken down. They needed Les to come and rescue them. Well, being the great guy that he is, Les got up, got dressed, and trudged out into the winter's night.

At that time, we lived on six hundred acres of wilderness at a Boy Scout reservation.

Brings back memories of my husband in those cute little shorts and that whistle, but hey, that's another story. Anyway, he trudged out into the night, leaving me and the young boys in the house alone, and that was fine with me. I had no problem with that, no fear—until our dog began to bark. Well, actually, I didn't even know it was our dog, and this is why: You see, our dog had a broken barker. I mean, she just didn't bark. We tried teaching her—now that's a sad thing, trying to teach your dog how to bark! But hark! When I heard the bark, I had to figure out what was going on, so I peeked out the window and what I saw from some of the light beams off the porch light was our dog, and her mouth was opening and closing in time with the bark. And I thought, "That is *our* dog, and it is barking."

Now, this concerned me, because I said to myself, "Self, what would cause a broken barker to suddenly kick in?" And I began to imagine . . . have you ever done that, just start imagining what might be? And I thought, "Well, perhaps it is an animal. Perhaps it's many animals. Perhaps it's a gaggle of animals." I mean, I could see herds moving in on the house. And then I thought, "Perhaps it's a thief—perhaps it's one of the scariest kinds of thieves, maybe one with *tattoos!*" [To Luci Swindoll:] Did I ever show you the butterfly on my ankle?

And the more I thought about what might be out there, the scarier it got until I scared myself half to death. And I got up and began looking for a weapon. Now, our house not only had a barkless dog, but it was a weaponless home. It wasn't something we ever had. In fact, I talked to a woman recently who verified to me why it was that we didn't keep them around. She said she heard a noise in the night, and she got up and got a loaded Colt .45. And as she pulled it out of the holster, her refrigerator motor kicked on—and she shot it! This is why we had no weapons.

So as I trudged through the house looking, I had to be fearless, creative. And then I saw it. I thought, "This will work." It was the Kirby vacuum cleaner. You know, those things are stout! They're sturdy. They're made to last forever. So I got the long, hard hose section, and I took it to bed with me.

I got into bed, and I was sitting up. I had my Kirby sword, and I was wielding it. And as I sat there I was watching. I was watching from the window to the door, the door to the window, the window to the door, and I turned my head too far and caught my reflection in the mirror . . . And I thought, "What's wrong with this picture?" Not looking like a woman of faith to me!

Then I thought, "I know what the problem is. I'm wielding the wrong kind of sword." So I laid down my Kirby sword, and I picked up the sword of the Spirit, which is the Word of God. I began to remind myself who God is and who he longs to be in my life. That he is my hiding place, my refuge, my tower of strength, the place that I go to in times of trouble. And as I reminded myself, I began to settle down. I actually became almost sane. And pretty soon I drifted off to sleep. I not only drifted off, I fell deeply asleep, and I know that, because I never heard my husband when he pulled up in front of the house. I didn't hear him when he came in the door. I didn't even hear him when he came into our bedroom—until he shook my foot and said, "What's the vacuum cleaner doing in bed with you?"

Patsy believes the best antidote to fear is _____.

Patsy describes her mind as a _____ of fear or a _____ of faith.

Patsy quotes Psalm 27:1, "The Lord is my light and my salvation; Whom shall I _____?" (We'll study this psalm later in the Back-Stage Pass segment.)

> *God not only saves me from my sins; he also saves me from myself.*
> —*Patsy*

Patsy's list of Bible "scaredy cats":

_____

_____

_____

Patsy's list of courageous Bible people:

_____

_____

_____

God wants us to know his boundless love, says Patsy. In boundless love there is also _____ love.

God is not reasonable.
—Patsy

We do not reason out God's ways because his ways are _____ _____ and his thoughts are _____.
(Note: We'll study Isaiah 55:8–9 in the Back-Stage Pass segment.)

Thoughts about divine confidence from the story Patsy told about taking her seven-year-old son Jason to the emergency room for stitches:

_____
_____
_____
_____
_____

Notes on the fear-of-flying story:

_____
_____
_____
_____
_____

He gave me three little words that unfolded inside my heart: In the beginning.
—Patsy

Notes on the osteoporosis story:

_____
_____
_____
_____
_____
_____
_____

Girls, may you know . . . that divine confidence that goes beyond reason so even in the midst of tragedy there is within you a confidence that others see and are drawn to you, realizing that it cannot be about you, it is all about him.
—Patsy

Taking It to Heart

Questions to help you personalize the lessons in the session

1. What do you tend to reach for when you are afraid?

   _____

   _____

2. Maybe you've never relied on a Kirby vacuum-cleaner hose for a sense of security . . . but what particularly lame choice for a weapon or protective device *have* you used in the past?

   _____

   _____

3. Patsy talks about the principle of divine confidence. How does she suggest we develop confidence in God's ability to take care of us no matter what the circumstances?

   _____

   _____

4. What did Patsy mean by the statement "God is not reasonable"?

_____

_____

I've said to the Lord on a number of occasions, "Lord, how can I communicate with other people about how frequently we need to be in the Word? I mean, when is it that we need to be in the Word?" He gave me three little words that unfolded inside my heart: *In the beginning.* So I went to Genesis, and I sat there. In the beginning, in the beginning, in the beginning. In the beginning of a new day, in the beginning of a conflict, in the beginning of hurt feelings, in the beginning of misunderstanding, in the beginning of hardship—in the beginning. Go into the Word of God and seek out his mind and his counsel. (Patsy)

5. Considering Patsy's message, what does the phrase "in the beginning" mean to you?

_____

_____

Taking It Home
Questions to help you apply the lessons in the session

1. Patsy talked about several major fears in her life (agoraphobia, fear of flying, and osteoporosis) and the lessons God has taught her through these fears. What are the major fears in your life at this moment?

   _____

   _____

2. If you could show Patsy the list you just made, what do you think, based on what she spoke about, she would say to you about your fears?

   _____

   _____

3. During what times or routines in your home, vehicles, and work could you benefit by having a Bible handy for reading?

   _____

   _____

4. In what ways do you want people in your Boundless Love group (or others) to keep you accountable for seeking continual exposure to God's Word in your life?

   _____

   _____

Back-Stage Pass—Bible Studies

Scripture passages used by Patsy Clairmont

Like the other Women of Faith speakers, Patsy bases her thoughts and analyzes her life experiences by the timeless truth from the Word of God.

If you're following the Fast-Track Option, skip this segment and go directly to A Last Word, encouraging your group members to use the Bible studies for review between sessions. If you're following the Full-Length Option, ask one of the women to read each passage aloud, then guide the group through the questions that follow. If time runs out, you may have to complete the Bible studies later at home. You'll have an opportunity during the Wrap-Up Session to share some of the insights you note here.

Psalm 27:1–14

The LORD is my light and my salvation;
Whom shall I fear?
The LORD is the strength of my life;
Of whom shall I be afraid?
²When the wicked came against me
To eat up my flesh,
My enemies and foes,
They stumbled and fell.
³Though an army may encamp against me,
My heart shall not fear;
Though war should rise against me,
In this I will be confident.

⁴One thing I have desired of the LORD,
That will I seek:
That I may dwell in the house of the LORD
All the days of my life,

To behold the beauty of the LORD,

And to inquire in His temple.

⁵For in the time of trouble

He shall hide me in His pavilion;

In the secret place of His tabernacle

He shall hide me;

He shall set me high upon a rock.

⁶And now my head shall be lifted up above my enemies all around me;

Therefore I will offer sacrifices of joy in His tabernacle;

I will sing, yes, I will sing praises to the LORD.

⁷Hear, O LORD, when I cry with my voice!

Have mercy also upon me, and answer me.

⁸When You said, "Seek My face,"

My heart said to You, "Your face, LORD, I will seek."

⁹Do not hide Your face from me;

Do not turn Your servant away in anger;

You have been my help;

Do not leave me nor forsake me,

O God of my salvation.

¹⁰When my father and my mother forsake me,

Then the LORD will take care of me.

¹¹Teach me Your way, O LORD,

And lead me in a smooth path, because of my enemies.

¹²Do not deliver me to the will of my adversaries;

For false witnesses have risen against me,

And such as breathe out violence.

¹³I would have lost heart, unless I had believed

That I would see the goodness of the LORD

In the land of the living.

[14]Wait on the LORD;
Be of good courage,
And He shall strengthen your heart;
Wait, I say, on the LORD!

Psalm 27 Study Questions

1. Read through the psalm and note next to each verse whether it has the past, present, or future in mind. What past circumstances trained David to "wait on the Lord"?

   _____

   _____

2. How do each of the following aspects of our relationship with God affect the way we face fears?

   God is our light.

   _____

   _____

   God is our salvation.

   _____

   _____

   God is the strength of our lives.

   _____

   _____

3. Verses 7–13 of this psalm record one of David's prayers. What specific requests did he make of God?

   _____

   _____

4. In what ways do David's requests represent your own desires as you struggle to be a woman of fearless faith?

_____

_____

_____

Isaiah 55

Ho! Everyone who thirsts,

Come to the waters;

And you who have no money,

Come, buy and eat.

Yes, come, buy wine and milk

Without money and without price.

²Why do you spend money for what is not bread,

And your wages for what does not satisfy?

Listen carefully to Me, and eat what is good,

And let your soul delight itself in abundance.

³Incline your ear, and come to Me.

Hear, and your soul shall live;

And I will make an everlasting covenant with you—

The sure mercies of David.

⁴Indeed I have given him as a witness to the people,

A leader and commander for the people.

⁵Surely you shall call a nation you do not know,

And nations who do not know you shall run to you,

Because of the LORD your God,

And the Holy One of Israel;

For He has glorified you.

⁶Seek the LORD while He may be found,

Call upon Him while He is near.

⁷Let the wicked forsake his way,

And the unrighteous man his thoughts;

Let him return to the LORD,

And He will have mercy on him;

And to our God,

For He will abundantly pardon.

⁸"For My thoughts are not your thoughts,

Nor are your ways My ways," says the LORD.

⁹"For as the heavens are higher than the earth,

So are My ways higher than your ways,

And My thoughts than your thoughts.

¹⁰"For as the rain comes down, and the snow from heaven,

And do not return there,

But water the earth,

And make it bring forth and bud,

That it may give seed to the sower

And bread to the eater,

¹¹So shall My word be that goes forth from My mouth;

It shall not return to Me void,

But it shall accomplish what I please,

And it shall prosper in the thing for which I sent it.

¹²"For you shall go out with joy,

And be led out with peace;

The mountains and the hills

Shall break forth into singing before you,

And all the trees of the field shall clap their hands.

¹³Instead of the thorn shall come up the cypress tree,

And instead of the brier shall come up the myrtle tree;

And it shall be to the LORD for a name,

For an everlasting sign that shall not be cut off."

Isaiah 55 Study Questions

A related thought from Patsy:

> For I have found, and I don't know about you, that God is not reasonable. I mean, I've seen it again and again unfold through the pages of Scripture. He does things differently than I would've done. I mean, even in my own life I think, "Whoops, I wonder if he knows about this. Surely he would've done it differently if he were aware . . ." Hello!! We cannot reason out God's ways because God's ways are above our ways and his thoughts are above our thoughts. . . . Go into the Word of God and seek his mind and counsel, for we cannot think up God's ways because they are so beyond us. If we are to know the fearless love of God, we must begin to saturate ourselves in his Word that we might have the weapons we would need mentally and emotionally to do the battle, not to give into some of the things that come into our thinking.

1. Twice in her presentation, Patsy alluded to Isaiah 55:8–9. In light of all Patsy said, explain why is it so important for us to agree with this statement: " 'For My thoughts are not your thoughts, nor are your ways My ways,' says the LORD. 'For as the heavens are higher than the earth, so are My ways higher than your ways, and My thoughts than your thoughts' "?

_____

_____

_____

_____

2. How many examples can you find in the first seven verses that illustrate the point that God's ways and thoughts are definitely not our ways or thoughts?

_____

_____

_____

3. Read verse 11 several times then reflect on why this verse is the central theme in this chapter of Isaiah.

_____

_____

_____

4. The last two verses of this chapter picture a life and a future full of joy and peace. Based on this chapter, in what ways does the presence of God's Word in our lives determine the degree of joy and peace that we experience?

_____

_____

_____

A Last Word
An insight from this session to remember until next time

Closing Thought. Patsy closes her talk with part of a letter written to her by a conference attendee during the time Patsy was dealing with her mother's Parkinson's and Alzheimer's. She uses it to encourage us to respond to God's boundless love during the very moments when we least feel like it. She wrote:

> "My daddy was an exceptional man. He'd been diagnosed with Parkinson's and Alzheimer's like your mama. And we watched as those diseases ravished his body and his mind—taking from us one memory after another. One day, my mama stepped into the room and my daddy was standing at the other end of the room. He was looking dazed. My mama asked him, 'Vernon, honey, what's the matter?'
>
> "And he turned to her and said, "I don't know who I am, but I know Jesus loves me.'"

Girls, may you know the boundless love of God regardless of the losses and the valleys that you may have to go through, regardless of how dry your old bones might get. No matter what the difficulty factor, remember he longs for you to know his boundless love—his fearless love.

THELMA WELLS:

God Loves You—
from Genesis to the Maps

Full-Length Option (90 minutes)

Introductions (5 minutes)

Welcome

Opening Prayer

Setting the Stage (Tape 1—2 minutes)

Main Event (Tape 2—35 minutes)

Taking It to Heart (15 minutes)

Taking It Home (15 minutes)

Back-Stage Pass—Bible Studies (15 minutes)

A Last Word and Closing Prayer (3 minutes)

Fast-Track Option (60 minutes)

Introductions (3 minutes)

Setting the Stage (Read the Welcoming Vignette script on your own before the session begins.)

Main Event (Tape 2—35 minutes)

Taking It to Heart (10 minutes)

Taking It Home (10 minutes)

Back-Stage Pass—Bible Studies (Complete these Bible studies later at your convenience.)

A Last Word and Closing Prayer (3 minutes)

Setting the Stage

Thelma's self-introduction offers us a glimpse of her vulnerability and a taste of her fascination with God's lavish love.

Thelma's Welcoming Vignette: Flower Power

I believe the most appreciated gift that a woman can get is the gift of flowers. My porch pals gave me a gift of a flower a month for twelve months, I think because they knew I had artificial plants in my yard . . . And some of those plants they gave me are still alive! Every time I look at those flowers, I think of the most ooey-gooey love story in the Bible. That love story is taken from the Song of Solomon.

Solomon says to his lover, "You are a flower in a beautiful garden."

And she says, "I'm just a lily of the valley; I'm just a rose of Sharon." What she really means is, "There's nothing really special about me."

But then Solomon says, "Oh, no! You are a rose among the thorns. You have captured my heart!" (Hmmmm, hmmmm, hmmmm!)

That's what God says to us, ladies. He says that we are beautiful flowers in a lovely garden, that we have captured his heart. This weekend we have a wonderful opportunity to hear about God's lavish love. The lavish love of God is the kind of love that doesn't hold anything from us. He loves us so much . . . that he just keeps on pouring, and keeps on giving, and keeps on spreading his love on us.

You know, his Son was called the Rose of Sharon, the Lily of the Valley. How wonderful it is to walk through green pastures and smell the aroma of God's grace and God's mercy, because he loves us.

Main Event

Leader's NOTES

Preview the video and complete the questions so you can anticipate your group members' responses. Remember to have the women read through this section quickly before viewing the video presentation to get a sense of Thelma's main points and so they're ready to jot down notes during the video showing.

Video Presentation by Thelma Wells: Yes! Jesus Loves Me!

How awesome it is to be in the presence of God and to understand that he loves us. And you know, I truly believe that if God could have a weakness (now, we know he doesn't), but if he *could* have a weakness, his weakness would be loving me and you. Am I right? That would be his weakness, because you see, he showers on us, not justice all the time, but he gives us mercy; he gives us grace; he gives us chance, after chance, after chance, after chance, after chance, after chance . . . Every morning there's a new day, he gives us another chance. And then, you can start your day over any time of the day. He gives us a new chance all the time. Yes! Jesus loves me!

I know Jesus loves me, because he has brought me a mighty, mighty, mighty long way—through all the problems and all the vicissitudes—he's even taught me something called "longsuffering"!

Now, I don't like longsuffering. But he has taught us—taught me, I don't know about you—loooooooooooooooongsuffering. That's one of the fruits. It's one we like to skip. We like the joy and the peace and the love and all that, but when it gets to longsuffering we mumble and grumble and then we go on to the next. But some of us are in stuff right now that we are suffering long. But have you noticed? Through all the longsuffering, through the lean times of our lives, which sometimes are mean times, but through all of those times, when we need him the most, he shows up. Isn't that good? When we need him the most, he shows up! Because Jesus loves us.

Thelma believes that one of the closest parallels to God's love for us is

_____

_____

Thelma conveys the intensity of her experience of being a mother when she says, "You can mess with my money, and some days you can mess with my honey, but on no days can you mess with my _____."

Like Sheila, Thelma reports that one of the lessons about herself that she has learned through her children, even her grown daughters, has been an awareness of her

_____

_____

Thelma quotes Jeremiah 29:11 to talk about her confidence that God has a _____

_____

_____

I thank God for not giving me some of the stuff I thought I wanted!

—Thelma

God had to teach Thelma that he is the Provider; everything else is a _____.

Notes on the lessons of being raised by her great-grandparents:

_____

_____

_____

_____

_____

We moved up when we moved to the projects!

—Thelma

Two passages of Scripture Thelma's great-grandfather taught her to repeat in the face of fear:

1. _____

2. _____

Have you ever known of a shadow that hurt anybody?

—Thelma

Thelma reports that the kind of fear that the Lord has removed by the use of his Word is what she calls _____ fear.

Notes on the Lord's Prayer:

_____

_____

_____

Scripture passages Thelma quotes:

If My people who are called by My name will humble them-selves, and pray and seek My face, and turn from their wicked ways, then I will hear from heaven, and will forgive their sin and heal their land. (2 Chronicles 7:14)

The Lord's Prayer is our protocol for entering into God's presence.

—Thelma

For we do not wrestle against flesh and blood, but against princi-palities, against powers, against the rulers of the darkness of this age, against spiritual hosts of wickedness in the heavenly places. Therefore take up the whole armor of God, that you may be able to withstand in the evil day, and having done all, to stand. (Ephesians 6:12–13)

> *From Genesis to the maps, he's telling us he loves us!*
>
> *—Thelma*

Notes on the story Thelma tells about her eighteen-year-old daughter's debutante party:

_____

_____

_____

_____

Taking It to Heart

Questions to help you personalize the lessons in the session

NOTES

Give the group a few moments to work on the following questions, then encourage participants to share personal illustrations that parallel Thelma's stories. Remind them that someone else in the group who may not be able to identify with a particular event in Thelma's life may connect with something that happened in theirs.

1. Describe your experiences with the phenomenon Thelma calls "mother mode."

_____

_____

2. Why do you think Thelma's great-grandfather's counsel about using Psalm 23 and the Lord's Prayer has such a powerful effect on Thelma's fears?

_____

_____

3. What's the difference between ordinary fear and what Thelma calls "lingering fear"?

_____

_____

4. Thinking about Thelma's story of how her daughter accepted her father's reluctance to say "I love you" and the way that opened a whole new freedom of communication in the family, how would you describe the effects of "acted-out love" and "verbally expressed love" in a family? Can they replace each other, or are both necessary?

_____

_____

5. How would you explain the meaning of the phrase Thelma quoted from Dwight Thompson: "We cannot do anything any more or any less to make God love us any more or any less"?

_____

_____

God loves you, and there's nothing you can do about it!

—Thelma

Taking It Home
Questions to help you apply the lessons in the session

Leader's NOTES

A significant part of Thelma's presentation was experiential—when she was singing and sharing her journaled thoughts from the Twenty-third Psalm and the Lord's Prayer. In addition to the following application questions, you may want to ask the women to reflect on what they were thinking/feeling while Thelma was singing. Ask if any of them keep a spiritual journal. What have they discovered through that personal discipline? What about singing when they're alone— has anyone experimented with that (other than in the shower)?

1. How would you respond if someone asked you, "How do you know God loves you?"

   _____

   _____

2. What are your favorite memorized (or familiar) passages of Scripture, and how do you use them in your daily life?

   _____

   _____

3. In the development of your relationship with God, what habits or practices have been most helpful in promoting a sense of intimacy between God and you?

   _____

   _____

4. As a result of observing Thelma speak, sing, and relate to the other women on the team, what character trait do you desire to make more obvious in your own life?

   _____

   _____

Leader's NOTES

If you are following the Fast-Track Option, direct the group now to A Last Word at the end of the session and encourage the women to complete the Bible studies later, at their convenience. If you're following the Full-Length Option, ask one of the women to read each passage aloud, then guide the group through the questions that follow. If time runs out, you may have to complete the Bible studies later at home. You'll have an opportunity during the Wrap-Up Session to share some of the insights you note here.

Thelma has illustrated a way of using memorized Scripture for devotional meditation. The practice requires that the person know the passage by heart. Ask if anyone in the group would be willing to honor the rest of you by sharing how memorized Scripture passages have helped her through a period of loooooooooooooooongsuffering.

Back-Stage Pass—Bible Studies

Scripture passages used by Thelma Wells

Psalm 23 (KJV)
A psalm of David

The LORD is my shepherd; I shall not want.

²He maketh me to lie down in green pastures: he leadeth me
beside the still waters.

³He restoreth my soul: he leadeth me in the paths of righteousness
for his name's sake.

⁴Yea, though I walk through the valley of the shadow of death, I
will fear no evil: for thou art with me; thy rod and thy staff
they comfort me.

⁵Thou preparest a table before me in the presence of mine enemies: thou anointest my head with oil; my cup runneth over.

⁶Surely goodness and mercy shall follow me all the days of my life:
and I will dwell in the house of the LORD forever.

Psalm 23 Study Questions

1. How many examples of God's boundless love can you identify in Psalm 23?

_____

_____

_____

2. Do we discover the Lord because he is our Shepherd, or do we discover the Shepherd when
we discover the Lord? (What is God's primary role: Lord or Shepherd?)

_____

_____

3. What word pictures or ideas in Psalm 23 do you find most comforting?

_____

_____

_____

4. If the Lord is our Shepherd, that makes us sheep. What specific attitudes in your life would bring out a more sheep-like character in you?

_____

_____

_____

Matthew 6:9–13 (KJV)

After this manner therefore pray ye:

Our Father which art in heaven,

Hallowed be thy name.

[10] Thy kingdom come.

Thy will be done in earth, as it is in heaven.

[11] Give us this day our daily bread.

[12] And forgive us our debts, as we forgive our debtors.

[13] And lead us not into temptation, but deliver us from evil:

For thine is the kingdom, and the power, and the glory, for ever. Amen.

Matthew 6:9–13 Study Questions

1. In what ways could our use of the Lord's Prayer be an acknowledgment of God's boundless love? _____

_____

_____

2. During what occasions are you most likely to use the Lord's Prayer, and what effect does it have on you?

_____

_____

3. What is the most vivid memory you have that involves the Lord's Prayer?

_____

_____

4. As part of your response as a woman of faith, in what areas of your life do you realize that you need to be more diligent about including prayer?

_____

_____

A Last Word

An insight from this session to remember until next time

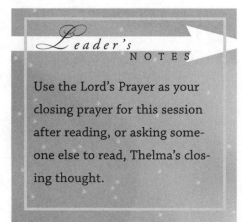

Leader's NOTES

Use the Lord's Prayer as your closing prayer for this session after reading, or asking someone else to read, Thelma's closing thought.

Closing Thought. The Lord's Prayer is our protocol for entering into the throne of grace. The Lord's Prayer says, "You don't have to have anybody to stand between you and me to get to me. You can walk right up to me." That's what he says. God says, "You can walk right up to me in the holy of holies, and you can come boldly before me, and I will hear you."

That's a good thing—that we don't need anybody else [to pray for us], that we can do it for ourselves.

BARBARA JOHNSON:

Getting What We Don't Deserve

Full-Length Option (90 minutes)

Introductions (5 minutes)

Welcome

Opening Prayer

Setting the Stage (Tape 1—2 minutes)

Main Event (Tape 2—12 minutes)

Taking It to Heart (15 minutes)

Taking It Home (15 minutes)

Back-Stage Pass—Bible Studies (15 minutes)

A Last Word and Closing Prayer (3 minutes)

Reflection and Discussion Time inserted into the session wherever it works best
for your group (25 minutes)

Fast-Track Option (60 minutes)

Introductions (5 minutes)

Setting the Stage (Tape 1—2 minutes)

Main Event (Tape 2—12 minutes)

Taking It to Heart (10 minutes)

Taking It Home (10 minutes)

Back-Stage Pass—Bible Studies (10 minutes—at least one passage)

A Last Word and Closing Prayer (3 minutes)

The Women of Faith conference during which these videos were made occurred under the shadow of Barbara Johnson's battle with a brain tumor. Thus she was not present during this taping session, but a shortened version of her previously recorded message was shown and is included here. While the other speakers' main presentations are thirty-five to forty-four minutes long, Barbara's presentation is only twelve minutes, so you will need to consider how you want to use the extra time in your session. We suggest that you include an extra twenty-five minutes of reflection and discussion if you're following the Full-Length Option and that you use the extra time to show the Welcoming Vignette and work through at least one question in Back-Stage Pass Bible Studies if you're following the Fast-Track Option.

One idea is to encourage a little longer time of sharing personal stories among the women. Barbara's Spatula Ministries is directed toward helping parents who "land on the ceiling" because of some heartbreaking crisis involving their children. Sometimes the heartache is caused by the child's homosexuality, estrangement, drug addiction, criminal activity, or even death. Barbara offers these parents a listening ear and a sympathetic heart. In the Spatula meetings, parents know they can talk about their children's problems in a loving, accepting atmosphere. If you feel comfortable that your group creates that kind of setting, ask any of the women who feel comfortable in doing so to talk about heartbreaking situations they've faced with their children and how they've survived. Be ready to respond to their words with love, sympathy, and prayers.

Setting the Stage

Leader's NOTES

Have Tape 1 cued to Barbara's Welcoming Vignette and Tape 2 cued to her main presentation. Tell the women that Barbara made the vignette recording a month after she had brain surgery for treatment of a malignant tumor. Because her head was shaved for the surgery, she is wearing one of the many "geranium hats" she has collected since the publication several years ago of her book *Stick a Geranium in Your Hat and Be Happy*. After viewing the Welcoming Vignette, proceed to Tape 2 to view her main presentation.

The Women of Faith conference during which these videos were made occurred under the shadow of Barbara Johnson's battle with cancer. Her illness was recognized from the start, and her encouraging remarks, made just a month after her craniotomy, had an uplifting effect on the gathering. As you'll see, her pithy storytelling and zany one-liners are priceless.

Barbara Johnson: Postsurgical Interview

I learned a long time ago [about choosing to be happy no matter what], and I wrote a book about it: *Stick a Geranium in Your Hat and Be Happy*. I think this time the book should be *Stick a Geranium in Your <u>Cranium</u> and Be Happy*.

When I had brain surgery, I didn't take a Tylenol; I didn't even have an aspirin. I didn't have any pain through the whole thing. That's because I have a numb skull.

I've lost my hair—but I haven't lost my humor!

This year we're talking about boundless love—God's boundless love. And even as I sit here with a brain tumor that is malignant, I know that God's love is wrapping me up, and his comfort blanket is around me.

I just said, "Well, Lord, you know what's come into my life. Everything has come in here through your filter. Nothing is a surprise to you." As long as he knows about it, I've got good doctors, I've got good friends that are praying for me, so I had to cast myself right on God's love and trust that he was going to get me through this. And he did.

The surgery was successful and they are going to be continuing to do some therapy on me for the next few weeks.

One of these days I'm going to be back with Women of Faith. Until then, I appreciate your prayers and your love.

Main Event

Leader's NOTES

When you preview the video, fill out the outline and blanks below. Think about your own initial responses to Barbara's comments because that will give you a headstart in anticipating how the women in your group will respond.

Preview the following section quickly to get a sense of Barbara's themes. This will alert you to her main points and help you prepare for jotting down notes during the video showing.

Video Presentation by Barbara Johnson:
A Lesson about Grace

The word *deserve* has a lot of special meaning for me, especially since I'm married to a man who likes to use that word. Now Bill—you probably met him last time—is almost perfect. They accuse me of being a man-basher because in my new book I have a chapter that says,

"If they can send a man to the moon . . . why can't they send 'em all?" But anyway, lest you think he is not wonderful, he is. He does everything navy-style—he makes the bed because he thinks I won't do it right. So I don't have to do that. And he puts gas in the car because he thinks I would spill it, and I probably would. And he's very low maintenance, because I don't have to cook. He just wants popcorn and hot dogs.

He never gets tickets. He always wears his seat belt. He's very compliant with the government. He always votes on time—he just does everything right. And when you live with someone like that . . . life isn't always really easy, even though I don't have many household chores, because he takes care of the ones he thinks I won't do right.

Sometime back I was getting ready to go speak and spread my joy somewhere. In the town where we live, La Habra, the post office is right next to the police station. There's a NO U-TURN sign right in front of the post office, but that's a dumb place to have it because that's where I always want to turn. And so, since I was in a hurry, I went past the post office, and I looked out and saw the sign, but I thought, *I've got to hurry and spread my joy,* so I just made a nice U-turn right in front of the police station and the post office.

Well, just as I had gotten around, straightening out the car, I looked in the mirror and here was a policeman coming behind me, and the light was going around and I thought, "Oh gosh!" So I pulled over and did what I know we're supposed to do in California (I have learned this from drivers school—they're acquainted with me there). You put your hands at 10 and at 2, pull over, roll down the window, and wait until they come up, and they are supposed to make the first remark. You don't talk to them until they talk to you. So I did that—rolled the window down and had my hands like this. And the policeman came up, and he didn't say a word. He just started pulling his gloves off, one finger at a time. And I wasn't about to say anything. I sat there, and he said, "Didn't you see that NO U-TURN sign?"

I said, "Well, I saw it, but I didn't think you really meant it."

He said, "We really meant it, sister." He wrote me out the ticket, and then I thanked him—always thank the officer. I put it in the glove compartment, and then I drove off. I only went two blocks down the road and looked in the mirror, and there he was, coming after me again. I mean, I hadn't done anything yet. I'd only gone two blocks! So I pulled over, rolled my window down, put my hands up on the wheel, and he came up—we went through the whole thing. Pulling off his gloves, he said, "Do you have the original ticket I gave you?"

I reached in the glove compartment and showed him the paper, and he said, "Don't you have the original?"

Well, I didn't eat it or anything! I thought, "This is really crazy."

So then he looked around the car, and he finally said, "All right, you can go." So I put the ticket back in the glove compartment where I had it, and I drove off thinking this must be something new in California. I knew it had been quite awhile—a few weeks—since I had gotten a ticket. I thought, "I'm never going to tell Bill because he never gets tickets or does anything wrong. I'll just go to AAA or someplace that will help me."

About ten days went by, and I was thinking, "I've got to do something about that ticket." In the mail came a letter addressed to William H. Johnson. It was from the La Habra Police Department. Well, that put him in a snit right there. So he opened up the letter. It had his driver's license number at the top and his name. And it said, "Dear Mr. Johnson, you can disregard the ticket that *you* got last week for the illegal U-turn" (he had a stroke right there) "because the original was lost."

He said, "Why, I—who . . . ?" Well, I wasn't about to relieve his guilt at all!

So, I just let him sweat for a while, and then I realized he was about to have a stroke, so I said, "I don't know. I showed them my license and my picture . . . how they got your name . . ." Right away, he said, "Well, you *deserve* it. You do that a lot. You're always doing that. You deserve the ticket . . ."

I don't want to hear what I deserve! If we all got what we deserve we ought to go down there [pointing downward]. It's only by God's grace that we don't . . .

But this was the most wonderful feeling. It's like being shot at and missed!

After she reads the letter from the woman who was part of a group attending one of the Women of Faith conferences in Texas, Barbara points out that the letter probably represents a cross section of the kind of _____ that is present when a group of women is gathered.

Barbara's outreach for parents is called Spatula Ministries because it is for parents who

_____

_____

Barbara knows she can't fix somebody else because she can't even _____

Notes on Barbara's comments on childrearing:

_____

_____

_____

_____

_____

> *I didn't cause it,*
> *I cannot control it, nor*
> *can I cure it; I can't*
> *fix anybody.*
>
> *—Barbara*

"To sum it up," says Barbara, "children come _____ us, not _____ us. Remember that, and realize that if there is no control, there's no responsibility."

> *The iron crown of*
> *suffering precedes the*
> *golden crown of glory.*
>
> *—Barbara*

Fill in the blanks in this Max Lucado poem Barb read:

If God had a _____, your picture would be on it.

If God had a _____, your photo would be in it.

He sends you flowers every spring, and a sunrise every morning.

When you want to talk, he'll _____.

He could live anywhere in the universe, and he chose your

_____.

And that Christmas gift he sent you in Bethlehem?

Face it, friend, he's _____ about you!

Taking It to Heart

Questions to help you personalize the lessons in the session

1. How did your awareness of Barbara's struggle with the brain tumor affect the way you listened and responded to her presentation?

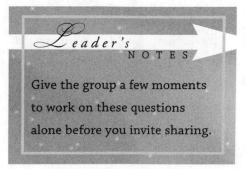

Leader's NOTES

Give the group a few moments to work on these questions alone before you invite sharing.

2. How would you describe Barbara's sense of humor? What tools does she use to encourage us to laugh?

_____

_____

3. In what ways did you feel that Barbara was providing you with a "balm from Gilead" for your life with her words?

_____

_____

4. What would you like to have heard more about from her among the topics she touched on in her brief remarks?

_____

_____

Leader's NOTES

Be aware that some of your group may identify closely with Barbara's suffering but feel resentful of her positive attitude or ashamed at their own inability to "rise above" their difficulties. Point out that Barbara has the benefit of a tremendous support group and that one of the best things that could come out of this study is a deeper sense of mutual accountability and caring between members of the group. Remind the women that lack of divine and human support and failing to ask God for help may be the most serious handicaps in facing almost any difficulty. As women mention struggles, invite others in the group to pray for them on the spot.

Taking It Home

Questions to help you apply the lessons in the session

1. What areas in your life make you most frequently a candidate for membership in one of Barbara's Spatula groups?

   _____

   _____

2. In what ways did you find Barbara's brief presentation a real encouragement in your life?

   _____

   _____

3. How do you relate to Barbara's reminder that we never get what we deserve?

   _____

   _____

4. In what ways have you most deeply experienced the reality of God's grace in your life?

   _____

   _____

Leader's NOTES

Because Barbara's message is brief, you should have time to discuss the Back-Stage Pass Bible studies, even if you're following the Fast-Track Option. Ask someone to read each passage aloud then work through the questions as a group (or divide into small groups if your gathering is large).

Back-Stage Pass—Bible Studies

Scripture passages used by Barbara Johnson

Psalm 103 (NIV)

Praise the LORD, O my soul;

    all my inmost being, praise his holy name.

2Praise the LORD, O my soul,

    and forget not all his benefits—

3who forgives all your sins

    and heals all your diseases,

4who redeems your life from the pit

    and crowns you with love and compassion,

5who satisfies your desires with good things

    so that your youth is renewed like the eagle's.

6The LORD works righteousness

    and justice for all the oppressed.

7He made known his ways to Moses,

    his deeds to the people of Israel:

8The LORD is compassionate and gracious,

    slow to anger, abounding in love.

9He will not always accuse,

    nor will he harbor his anger forever;

10he does not treat us as our sins deserve

    or repay us according to our iniquities.

¹¹For as high as the heavens are above the earth,

    so great is his love for those who fear him;

¹²as far as the east is from the west,

    so far has he removed our transgressions from us.

¹³As a father has compassion on his children,

    so the LORD has compassion on those who fear him;

¹⁴for he knows how we are formed,

    he remembers that we are dust.

¹⁵As for man, his days are like grass,

    he flourishes like a flower of the field;

¹⁶the wind blows over it and it is gone,

    and its place remembers it no more.

¹⁷But from everlasting to everlasting

    the LORD'S love is with those who fear him,

    and his righteousness with their children's children—

¹⁸with those who keep his covenant

    and remember to obey his precepts.

¹⁹The LORD has established his throne in heaven,

    and his kingdom rules over all.

²⁰Praise the LORD, you his angels,

    you mighty ones who do his bidding,

    who obey his word.

²¹Praise the LORD, all his heavenly hosts,

    you his servants who do his will.

²²Praise the LORD, all his works

    everywhere in his dominion.

Praise the LORD, O my soul.

Psalm 103 Study Questions

1. How many times is the phrase "praise the Lord" used in this psalm, and who is invited to respond this way?

   _____

   _____

2. Verse 2 mentions "benefits," and the rest of the psalm mentions many of these. How many benefits can you identify that the psalmist realized God provides?

   _____

   _____

3. What examples of boundless love can you list in this psalm? In particular, how would you explain verse 8?

   _____

   _____

4. How does Psalm 103:10, the verse Barbara quotes at the beginning of her talk, apply to your own experience of God's boundless love?

   _____

   _____

5. What personal reasons would you give for being willing to "praise the Lord," as both the first and last verses of this psalm invite you to do?

   _____

   _____

Ephesians 2:1–10

And you He made alive, who were dead in trespasses and sins, ²in which you once walked according to the course of this world, according to the prince of the power of the air, the spirit who now works in the sons of disobedience, ³among whom also we all once conducted ourselves in the lusts of our flesh, fulfilling the desires of the flesh and of the mind, and were by nature children of wrath, just as the others.

⁴But God, who is rich in mercy, because of His great love with which He loved us, ⁵even when we were dead in trespasses, made us alive together with Christ (by grace you have been saved), ⁶and raised us up together, and made us sit together in the heavenly places in Christ Jesus, ⁷that in the ages to come He might show the exceeding riches of His grace in His kindness toward us in Christ Jesus. ⁸For by grace you have been saved through faith, and that not of yourselves; it is the gift of God, ⁹not of works, lest anyone should boast. ¹⁰For we are His workmanship, created in Christ Jesus for good works, which God prepared beforehand that we should walk in them.

Ephesians 2:1–10 Study Questions

1. In her presentation, Barbara contrasted "what we deserve" with God's grace. Based on the language in these verses, how would you describe grace?

   _____

   _____

2. Write out a personalized version of verse 8 in which you specifically replace the three words *grace*, *saved*, and *faith* with a word or phrase that explains what those words mean to you.

   _____

   _____

3. In verses 8 and 9, how does the phrase "not of works" fit into the way that God treats us?

   _____

   _____

   _____

4. In what personal ways do you believe these verses apply to your life?

_____

_____

A Last Word
An insight from this session to remember until next time

Leader's NOTES

Take time to read Barbara's closing thought before you end the session with prayer. Invite the group to pray for one another again, perhaps reflecting on some of the sharing that has gone on during the session. Ask one or two women to pray for the ministry of Women of Faith, and particularly for Barbara Johnson. Before you dismiss the group after prayer, briefly review what the women will need to do in preparation for the next session.

Closing Thought. Sometimes people will say, "I don't know why I have to go through this trial. I mean, why do I have to have lost my child and have this happen? Why should I have that?"

Well, God will take that trial and use it to make you more fine-tuned, to make you a better counselor, a better person, and closer to the Lord—because you have been through the fires. The iron crown of suffering precedes the golden crown of glory. And when you go through that, it's going to make you so much more improved and fine-tuned!

Outlandish Love

MARILYN MEBERG:

Surviving Those Whale-Belly Experiences

Full-Length Option (90 minutes)

Introductions (5 minutes)

Welcome

Opening Prayer

Setting the Stage (Tape 1—2 minutes)

Main Event (Tape 2—44 minutes)

Taking It to Heart (15 minutes)

Taking It Home (15 minutes)

Back-Stage Pass—Bible Studies (Assigned homework)

A Last Word and Closing Prayer (3 minutes)

Fast-Track Option (60 minutes)

Introductions (3 minutes)

Setting the Stage (Read the Welcoming Vignette script on your own before the session begins.)

Main Event (Tape 2—44 minutes)

Taking It to Heart (10 minutes)

Taking It Home (10 minutes)

Back-Stage Pass—Bible Studies (Complete these Bible studies later at your convenience.)

A Last Word and Closing Prayer (2 minutes)

Setting the Stage

Like several of her teammates, Marilyn enjoys the role of grandmother. This passage of her life has provided her with many new adventures and stories. She introduces herself to the Boundless Love audience with this vignette about her grandson Alec and a lesson in God's unconditional love.

Marilyn's Welcoming Vignette: Isn't She Beautiful?

Alec is in love. Alec is talking about marriage. Alec is three years old. So too is his fiancée. Wanting to enter into this as best I could as his grandmother, I started talking about the wedding.

He said to me, "Grandma, you can't come."

"I'm your grandmother!"

"I'm sorry, Grandma. You're too old."

"Well, how old do you have to be to come to the wedding?"

"Three."

I was picking him up after preschool a couple of days ago, and as I was getting ready to buckle him into his car seat, he said to me, "Look! There's Allison! There she is!"

This was his betrothed.

I said, "Really?"

He said, "Do you want to meet her?"

I said, "Well, yes!" I knew I wouldn't see her any other time.

And so he hollered out the window, "Allison, come meet my grandma!" She backed out of the minivan in which she was about to get in, and when she turned around, I was stunned. The most unattractive little child I'd ever seen! There was a little something wrong with *everything* about her.

As I was buckling Alec into his seat, he said, "Grandma, isn't she *beautiful?*"

God said something to me in that. "You know, Marilyn," he said, "there's a little something wrong with everything about you. And oh, Marilyn, you are beautiful. Absolutely beautiful."

We come this weekend to hear about God's outrageous, outlandish, never-ending love that sweeps over us without criticism, without condemnation. And you will leave here with his words echoing in your head, "She's beautiful. She's beautiful."

Main Event

Marilyn's presentation certainly fits her topic. She is an outlandishly delightful speaker who enjoys speaking about the outlandish love of God!

Video Presentation by Marilyn Meberg:
Beyond the Walled Community

Notes on Marilyn and Luci's golf-cart adventure:

_____

_____

Marilyn loved that golf-cart adventure because it was _____!

Words Marilyn uses to define or explain "outlandish":

_____

_____

Biblical examples of God's outlandish actions:

Jericho _____

_____

Goliath _____

_____

Noah _____

_____

Ezekiel _____

_____

Eve _____

_____

The explanatory sentence in Scripture for God's outlandish acts: "That ye might know that I am _____."

Notes on Marilyn's outlandish rescue in the desert:

_____

_____

_____

Notes on Jonah's rescue mission:

_____

_____

_____

_____

Have you ever been in a whale belly?

—Marilyn

The first response to a whale-belly experience is to _____.

Whale-Belly Scripture verses—First Response: (We'll study these passages in the Back-Stage Pass Bible Studies segment.)

John 16:24

_____

_____

_____

Jesus said, "Use my name." There is power in the name of God.
—Marilyn

Isaiah 52:6

_____

_____

_____

Jeremiah 10:6

_____

_____

_____

The second response to a whale-belly experience is to _____.

Remember, there's always a rescue plan!

—Marilyn

Whale-Belly Scripture verses—Second Response: (We'll study these passages in the Back-Stage Pass Bible Studies.)

Psalm 41:1

_____

_____

_____

Proverbs 23:18

_____

_____

_____

Psalm 30:5

_____

_____

_____

Notes on the outlandish parts of God's plan in the life of Jesus:

_____

_____

Notes on Marilyn's description of what happens when we "come to the cross":

_____

_____

Taking It to Heart
Questions to help you personalize the lessons in the session

1. What does Marilyn say is the central lesson she has learned from God's outlandish acts?

_____

_____

2. How did she describe the outlandish part of her second desert rescue?

_____

_____

3. What do you think Marilyn meant by her question, "Have you ever been in a whale belly?"

_____

_____

4. Marilyn recommends two significant basic responses that a person ought to practice if she wants to witness the outlandish love of God in action:

Step 1: _____

_____

Step 2: _____

_____

5. How do *you* understand Marilyn's emphasis on the name of Jesus?

_____

_____

Leader's NOTES

This session may be the best opportunity during the Boundless Love study to get a sense of the spiritual maturity of your group. Marilyn presents the gospel in a win- some way and invites a response. As noted previously in Leader's Notes, the responses by your group members will probably influ- ence the direction of your discussion.

Taking It Home

Questions to help you apply the lessons in the session

1. What story or event in your life would you most likely use as an example of God's outlandish love toward you?

   _____

   _____

2. What was your most recent whale-belly experience?

   _____

   _____

3. How did you use Marilyn's two responses—praying and remembering? What difference did they make? (If you didn't use them because you didn't know about them, what difference do you think they would have made?)

   _____

   _____

4. Using Marilyn's picture of coming to the cross in the name of Jesus, what location most clearly describes your relationship with Jesus right now?

   _____ Where's the cross?

   _____ I can see the cross, but it's a long way from me.

   _____ I am definitely moving toward the cross.

   _____ I'm closer to the cross of Jesus than I have ever been before.

   _____ I've still got some major obstacles between myself and the cross.

   _____ I feel like I've just arrived at the cross, where I've found boundless love.

   _____ I live by the cross.

5. Reflect a little on why you chose your particular answer above.

_____

_____

6. If you could ask the rest of the group to pray for you about one thing concerning your relationship with Jesus, what would that be?

_____

_____

Back-Stage Pass—Bible Studies
Scripture passages used by Marilyn Meberg

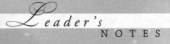

First Response When You Find Yourself in a Whale Belly: Call on the Name of Jesus

John 16:24

Until now you have asked nothing in My name. Ask, and you will receive, that your joy may be full.

Isaiah 52:6

> Therefore My people shall know My name;
>
> Therefore they shall know in that day
>
> That I am He who speaks:
>
> "Behold, it is I."

Jeremiah 10:6

> Inasmuch as there is none like You, O LORD
>
> (You are great, and Your name is great in might).

First Response Study Questions

1. How does someone's knowing or not knowing your name affect your relationship with that person?

   _____

   _____

   _____

2. Based on Marilyn's explanation and your reading of the passages above, what are the privileges and the power connected with God's name?

   _____

   _____

   _____

3. In what specific ways do you use the name of the Lord as part of your personal interaction with him?

   _____

   _____

   _____

Second Response:
Remember the Promises of Protection

Psalm 41:1

> Blessed is he who considers the poor;
> The LORD will deliver him in time of trouble.

Proverbs 23:18

> For surely there is a hereafter,
> And your hope will not be cut off.

Psalm 30:5

> For His anger is but for a moment,
> His favor is for life;
> Weeping may endure for a night,
> But joy comes in the morning.

Second Response Study Questions

1. Are there other passages from Scripture you can think of that highlight God's promises?

   _____

   _____

2. In what ways does God's faithfulness in your own past help you deal with the challenges of the present and future?

   _____

   _____

3. In what area of your life would it make the biggest difference if you could match God's outlandish possibilities with an outlandish trust that, to use Marilyn's phrase, "there's always a rescue plan"?

A Last Word

An insight from this session to remember until next time

I'd like to invite you now . . . if you have never come to the cross and said, "Lord Jesus, I do want to be rescued from who I am, from the sin within me, from the mess I've gotten in. I've been in so many whale bellies I hardly know what it's like to breathe free air. I need to be rescued," would you bow your head with me and pray very simply:

"Lord Jesus, I want to be a Christian. I want you to come in right now, this minute, and clean me up. I repent, ask forgiveness for, and make confession of the messes I've made. Jesus, forgive me. Forgive me! Thank you that at this very minute you will come in to me, cleanse me, and receive me now as a member of the eternal family of God. Thank you. Amen."

And now, if you prayed that prayer, do you know what's happening this minute in the heavenlies? Jesus is taking you and walking you over to God the Father, and he's saying, "Here she is, cleansed, forgiven. She's your daughter."

And God says, "Isn't she beautiful!"

At this point in the conference, Women of Faith president Mary Graham asks the women in the auditorium to remain quietly in their seats in consideration of those who are making this life-changing decision. She asks them to fill out a response card similar to the form provided here. At the bottom of the form is a little box. "It looks like a mistake," Mary says, "but it's not." If you have made the decision today to accept Jesus as your personal Savior, we want to hear from you! Please photocopy the form that follows, provide the information requested, then *check the box* and mail the form to us at

Decision

Women of Faith

820 W. Spring Creek Parkway, Suite 400

Plano, TX 75023

We'll celebrate your decision by sending you a free copy of the New Testament!

Date: _____

Name: _____

Address: _____

_____

_____

E-mail address: _____

Tell us how you're using the *Boundless Love Women of Faith Interactive and Application Guide:*

_____ On my own

_____ In a group associated with _____

_____

(the name and address of the church or other organization that's sponsoring your sessions)

❏

Marilyn continues:

It's a sobering thing—we talk about using the name of Jesus. That's for family members. No one has access to that name unless they have come to the cross and asked Jesus to come into their interior being and cleanse them and forgive them of sin. He then has become their Father. They (you and I) are then entitled to use the name. Otherwise, you will notice that it is a name for cursing—not for praising, not for family membership. Come to the cross and say again, "Lord Jesus, I do want to be rescued from who I am, from the sin within me, from the mess I've gotten in. I've been in so many whale bellies I hardly know what it's like to breathe free air! I need to be rescued."

The attitude and prayer that served Jonah so well so long ago will serve you just as well, every moment and anywhere.

Intentional Love

LUCI SWINDOLL:

Going God's Way
(Whether We Like It or Not)

Full-Length Option (90 minutes)

Introductions (5 minutes)

Welcome

Opening Prayer

Setting the Stage (Tape 1—2 minutes)

Main Event (Tape 3—40 minutes)

Taking It to Heart (10 minutes)

Taking It Home (15 minutes)

Back-Stage Pass—Bible Studies (15 minutes)

A Last Word and Closing Prayer (3 minutes)

Fast-Track Option (60 minutes)

Introductions (3 minutes)

Setting the Stage (Read the Welcoming Vignette script on your own before the session begins.)

Main Event (Tape 3—40 minutes)

Taking It to Heart (10 minutes)

Taking It Home (10 minutes)

Back-Stage Pass—Bible Studies (Complete these Bible studies later at your convenience.)

A Last Word and Closing Prayer (2 minutes)

Setting the Stage

Luci's Welcoming Vignette: Scenes from a Grocery Store

About nine o'clock one night, I went down to the grocery store to get a few things before bedtime. I walked in and there weren't very many people there. The guy in front of me at the checkout stand was very, very handsome. I noticed him, of course. He looked kind of like Pete Sampras; you know, dark, kind face with beauti—well anyway, very good looking. The only problem was, ladies, he was covered with tattoos. (Groan) Yeah, that's kind of what I thought, too. Ugh. And I was sort of mildly offended. I'm not much one for tattoos. As I looked at him, I thought, "Well, he looks really more like a rag rug than a person—covered with tattoos—Pete Sampras in a rag rug." So, in my mind, I named him Rag Rug Pete.

He had with him a little baby in a kind of a bassinet attached to the cart that he was putting his groceries in, and a toddler who was walking along by him. I thought, "This guy is covered with tattoos. Now, he is a thief or he wouldn't have those tattoos. And I'm going to see him on the eleven o'clock news. He has probably robbed the local bank right down there—not only that, but he has kidnapped those kids." I had it figured out! And so I kept my eye on him.

We got up to the checkout stand. The gal who was sacking his groceries knew him, and I thought, "They're in cahoots here, you know. She's his partner in crime."

She said, "How are you doing?"

He said, "Great."

She said, "Where's your wife tonight?"

He said, "Well, I gave her the evening off because she worked all day. I just thought I could help her. So I grabbed the kids and came on down."

I thought, "Well, he's kind of cute . . . he's getting cuter, you know." About this time, he took the baby out of the little bassinet and just held the baby. He stroked the baby and hugged the little toddler . . . Now he was getting cuter by the minute! I thought, "Well, maybe he's not quite as bad as I thought."

As I was leaving and going to my car, I was chiding myself for being so judgmental. I thought, "Luci, you little creep. Here you are, judging him because he has tattoos." And I thought, "Aren't you glad that God doesn't label you?"

And aren't you ladies glad that God doesn't label you? He doesn't look at you and say, "You're fat, or you're old, or you smoke, or you have tattoos." He says, "I love you! I don't label you. I love you!" This weekend, I'm talking about the intentional love of God. He loves you unconditionally. He loves you on purpose.

Main Event

Leader's NOTES

Once again, ask group members to take a moment to review the notetaking spaces on the following pages before viewing the video so they can be aware of the main points and are ready to jot down notes during the video showing.

Video Presentation by Luci Swindoll:
On Having a Wonderful Father

My father was a wonderful man. He was tall and handsome. He was a good caretaker, a good provider. I loved him with all my heart until the day he died. In the words of Marilyn Meberg, I used to think he was the fourth person of the Trinity. Daddy used to say to me, "You can do anything you want to do. You can be anything you want to be. You can go anywhere you want to go. All you need to do is line your will with the will of God, and you can do it. You can do anything." And I believed it. He was just such an encourager and a cheerleader. When I had problems, I would go to Daddy because he was my hero. Who doesn't want a father like that?

If you have your faith in Jesus Christ, you *have* a Father just like that. You can do anything you want to do. You can be anything you want to be. Nothing is impossible with him. You can go anywhere. You can do it in the power of his love and might. The world is your oyster because God made the oyster and you belong to him. He is great.

I thought of that old hymn not long ago that says, "Oh, the deep, deep love of Jesus, vast, unmeasured, boundless, free. Rolling as a mighty ocean in its fullness over me. Underneath me, all around me is the current of Thy love; Leading onward, leading homeward to my glorious rest above." Underneath me, around me is the boundless current of God's love telling me I can do anything, as can you. You can get out of the mirey clay that you're in. He can put your feet on a rock. He can put a song in your mouth. He can lift your spirit because HE IS GOD and he loves you, and he loves me, and he loves us whether we win or we lose. That's one of my favorite things about him.

The Five Fingers of Finance

1. _____
2. _____
3. _____
4. _____
5. _____

It helps when you grow old to take everything as a compliment.

—Luci

Luci tells a hilarious story about the misadventures she experienced on a well-planned trip to France she took with Mary Graham. She explains her attitude this way:

> I'm not real good at losing. I like to win. I *plan* on winning. I am the last of the big-time planners. And if things thwart my plans, I have a problem with that. If God comes in and says to me, "My plan is better than your plan," . . . I have a problem with that!

Notes on winning/planning/traveling:

_____

_____

_____

_____

Luci asks: "Why am I telling you this story?" Describe her answer.

_____

_____

_____

Proverbs 3:5–8 (MSG)

Trust God from the bottom of your heart. Don't try to figure out everything on your own. Listen for God's voice in everything you do and everywhere you go. He's the one that will keep you on track. Don't assume that you know it all. Run to God; run from evil. Your body will glow with health, your very bones will vibrate with life.

> *I am so glad that when I misbehave God doesn't get me because I am a jerk!*
>
> —*Luci*

Taking It to Heart

Questions to help you personalize the lessons in the session

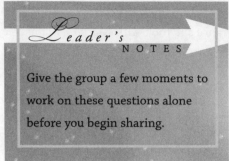

Leader's NOTES

Give the group a few moments to work on these questions alone before you begin sharing.

1. In what ways did Luci's stories convey a sense of God's intentional love to you?

   _____

   _____

   _____

2. Given Luci's struggles with disappointment over foiled plans, what do you think is the role of planning in our relationship with God?

   _____

   _____

3. What was the one condition Luci's dad mentioned that affects our success in doing anything we want to do? (See Luci's video presentation script, page 82.)

   _____

   _____

4. After Luci quotes Proverbs 3:5–8 from *The Message,* she comments: "You are so alive because you have run to God; you have trusted him. I can tell you—it's the hardest thing in the world. And it's the only thing that gives us full reward in him. Trust in God." Luci then uses the Van Gogh painting to illustrate trust. What picture, story, or idea do you use to illustrate what it means to trust?

   _____

   _____

5. Luci reads Psalm 119:32 (NIV), which says, "I run in the path of your commands because you have set my heart free." The only way we can run to God, she says, is if we have a free heart. "We are the children. God is the Father. I can say from my own experience, it is not until we learn that lesson that we can walk in peace with God and feel all the love he has for us." Without missing any planes and falling down an escalator, how have *you* learned that lesson?

_____

_____

_____

_____

_____

_____

Taking It Home

Questions to help you apply the lessons in the session

Leader's NOTES

Note how open-ended Luci makes her presentation. In somewhat of a contrast to Marilyn's "arrival at the cross" message, Luci follows with a "going on from here" challenge, reminding us that, even after years of faithfulness, the pathway of trust in God does not lack its stumbling blocks.

1. When Luci told you why she was telling her embarrassing stories—because we're all like that—what episode or habit in your life came to mind?

_____

_____

2. How do you tend to respond when God overrules, adjusts, or seems to ignore your plans?

_____

_____

3. How would you describe the central lesson or challenge about trusting God in your life that came to you through Luci (or any of the other speakers)?

_____

_____

_____

4. How do you think trust goes together with boundless love when it comes to God?

_____

_____

_____

Back-Stage Pass—Bible Studies

Scripture passages used by Luci Swindoll

Leader's NOTES

If you are following the Fast-Track Option, direct the group to A Last Word at the end of the session and encourage the women to complete the Bible studies later, at their convenience. After allowing the group to read these passages silently and work on the questions a few moments alone or in small groups, have someone read each passage aloud before you discuss it.

Proverbs 3:5–8

Trust in the LORD with all your heart,
And lean not on your own understanding;
⁶In all your ways acknowledge Him,
And He shall direct your paths.

⁷Do not be wise in your own eyes;
Fear the LORD and depart from evil.
⁸It will be health to your flesh,
And strength to your bones.

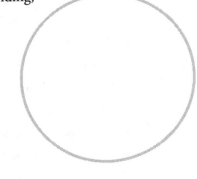

Proverbs 3:5–8 Study Questions

1. What part of trusting the Lord do you find most difficult? (Refer also to the earlier quotation of this passage from *The Message*.)

_____

_____

_____

2. What does "acknowledging" actually mean? In what ways have you or haven't you been acknowledging him?

_____

_____

_____

3. How would you connect the idea of trusting God with the possibility of healthy living?

_____

_____

_____

Romans 8:18–28

For I consider that the sufferings of this present time are not worthy to be compared with the glory which shall be revealed in us. [19]For the earnest expectation of the creation eagerly waits for the revealing of the sons of God. [20]For the creation was subjected to futility, not willingly, but because of Him who subjected it in hope; [21]because the creation itself also will be delivered from the bondage of corruption into the glorious liberty of the children of God. [21]For we know that the whole creation groans and labors with birth pangs together until now. [23]Not only that, but we also who have the firstfruits of the Spirit, even we ourselves groan within ourselves, eagerly waiting for the adoption, the redemption of our body. [24]For we were saved in this hope, but hope that is seen is not hope; for why does one still hope for what he sees? [25]But if we hope for what we do not see, we eagerly wait for it with perseverance.

[26]Likewise the Spirit also helps in our weaknesses. For we do not know what we should pray for as we ought, but the Spirit Himself makes intercession for us with groanings which cannot be uttered. [27]Now He who searches the hearts knows what the mind of the Spirit is, because He makes intercession for the saints according to the will of God.

[28]And we know that all things work together for good to those who love God, to those who are the called according to His purpose.

Romans 8:18–28 Study Questions

1. When Luci quoted this last verse (Romans 8:28), many in the audience quoted it with her. People are often unfamiliar with the context. Given what precedes it, would you say that Paul led up to this promise with hardships or comfort on his mind?

   _____

   _____

2. What phrases from these eleven verses would you highlight as being particularly descriptive of your life?

   _____

   _____

3. In what ways does verse 28 respond to questions like this: Why is this bad thing happening to me? Why aren't my plans working out?

_____

_____

4. If we have God's promise to work out everything for our good, why do we get so upset when our plans get sidetracked?

_____

_____

5. In what specific area or way are you determined to trust or acknowledge God more intentionally in the future? Why?

_____

_____

A Last Word

An insight from this session to remember until next time

Leader's NOTES

After you share Luci's closing thought, end this session with a special time of prayer. Enjoy the deeper level of sharing and intimacy that has developed as you have explored God's boundless love together.

Closing Thought. We are the children. God is the Father. I can say from my own experience, it is not until we learn that lesson that we can walk in peace with God and feel all the love he has for us. Ladies, God's love is boundless! It is fearless! It is lavish! It is stubborn! It is outlandish! And he is intentional about every bit of that. And it is for you and for me—and we can take that to the bank!

SHEILA WALSH:

Little Gifts of Love to Take Home

Like the Introductory Session, the Wrap-Up Session is intentionally unscripted so you can use the allotted time in the way that works best for you or your group. Before the session begins, cue Tape 3 to Sheila's fifteen-minute wrap-up message.

Open the session with prayer, thanking God for the time you've spent together, the opportunities you've had to learn more about his boundless, fearless, lavish, stubborn, outlandish, intentional love. Ask a group member to read aloud again the verse from Ephesians 5 at the end of "His Love Never Ends" on page v. Next, show Sheila's fifteen-minute wrap-up message.

Use the remainder of the time to share what you've learned during the last seven sessions. Go through the sessions one by one, inviting participants to review their notes and briefly share interesting insights they've gained. This is also a good time to review the Back-Stage Pass Bible Studies notes, as well.

You might say, "Let's go back and quickly review our notes then share some of the highlights of these sessions. We'll begin with Sheila's message on boundless love. As you look back through your notes on this message, tell us one favorite truth you learned or one change you made in your life because of something you discovered during this session. Be sure to look through your notes on the Bible studies as well as Sheila's message."

Next, remember that at the beginning of the series you discussed what God's boundless love meant to you. Ask each woman how her perception of God's love has changed. You could also ask the women to consider which of the "little gifts" from the speakers, described in Sheila's wrap-up remarks, they will find most useful as reminders of God's love in their lives.

The kind of interaction you have over these questions will give you a good indication of what might be a good follow-up study.

Close with prayer and ask God's blessings upon your lives as you take his love into the world.

Sharing the Blessings

What are the little gifts the speakers have sent you as mementos of this series?

Sheila's gift: _____

It reminds you that _____

_____

_____

_____

_____

Patsy's gift: _____

It reminds you that _____

_____

_____

_____

_____

Thelma's gift: _____

It reminds you that _____

_____

_____

_____

_____

Barbara's gift: _____

It reminds you that _____

_____

_____

_____

_____

Marilyn's gift: _____

It reminds you that _____

_____

_____

_____

_____

Luci's gift: _____

It reminds you that _____

_____

_____

_____

_____

NOTES

NOTES

NOTES

NOTES

More than 1.6 million women will gather to change one life . . .

yours.

Sheila WALSH

Barbara JOHNSON

Marilyn MEBERG

Patsy CLAIRMONT

Thelma WELLS

Luci SWINDOLL

Join us with your friends at a Women of Faith conference for two days of fellowship, worship, tears, and joy as amazing speakers share from their hearts about the power of living a life overflowing with the love of God.

> Sensational Life 2002 Dates*

February 22–23
Cincinnati, OH
Firstar Center

April 5–6
Kansas City, MO
Kemper Arena

April 12–13
Sacramento, CA
Arco Arena

May 3–4
Shreveport, LA
CenturyTel Center

May 31–June 1
Spokane, WA
Spokane Arena

June 3–10
Alaskan Cruise

June 14–15
Birmingham, AL
BJCC Arena

June 21–22
Charleston, SC
N. Charleston Coliseum

June 28–29
Cleveland, OH
Gund Arena

July 12–13
Chicago, IL
United Center

July 19–20
Toronto, ON, Canada
Air Canada Centre

July 26–27
St. Louis, MO
Savvis Center

August 2–3
Ft. Lauderdale, FL
National Car Rental Ctr

August 9–10
Dallas, TX
American Airlines Center

August 16–17
Washington, DC
MCI Center

August 23–24
Denver, CO
Pepsi Center

September 6–7
Anaheim, CA
Arrowhead Pond

September 20–21
Hartford, CT
Hartford Civic Center

September 27–28
Philadelphia, PA
First Union Center

October 4–5
Charlotte, NC
Charlotte Coliseum

October 11–12
Detroit, MI
Palace of Auburn Hills

October 18–19
Houston, TX
Compaq Center

October 25–26
Portland, OR
Rose Garden Arena

November 1–2
Orlando, FL
TD Waterhouse Centre

November 8–9
Ames, IA
Hilton Coliseum

November 15–16
San Jose, CA
Compaq Center at San Jose

> Great Adventure 2003 Dates*

February 21–22
Sacramento, CA
Arco Arena

March 14–15
Memphis, TN
Pyramid Arena

March 28–29
Columbus, OH
Nationwide Arena

April 4–5
Kansas City, MO
Kemper Arena

April 25–26
Vancouver, BC, Canada
General Motors Arena

May 2–3
Shreveport, LA
CenturyTel Center

May 16–17
Louisville, KY
Freedom Hall

May 30–31
Billings, MT
MetraPark

June 13–14
Charleston, SC
N. Charleston Coliseum

June 20–21
Ft. Lauderdale, FL
National Car Rental Ctr

June 27–28
Toronto, ON, Canada
Air Canada Centre

July 11–12
Dallas, TX
America Airlines Ctr

July 18–19
Washington, DC
MCI Center

July 25–26
Denver, CO
Pepsi Center

August 1–2
Atlanta, GA
Philips Arena

August 8–9
Oklahoma City, OK
Myriad Arena

August 15–16
Ames, IA
Hilton Coliseum

August 22–23
Chicago, IL
United Center

September 5–6
Anaheim, CA
Arrowhead Pond

September 12–13
St. Paul, MN
Xcel Energy Center

September 19–20
Albany, NY
Pepsi Arena

September 26–27
Detroit, MI
Palace of Auburn Hills

October 10–11
Portland, OR
Rose Garden Arena

October 24–25
Charlotte, NC
Charlotte Coliseum

October 31–Nov.1
Omaha, NE
MECA

November 7–8
Philadelphia, PA
First Union Center

November 14–15
Orlando, FL
TD Waterhouse Centre

For more information call **1-888-49-faith**
or visit us on the Web at **www.womenoffaith.com**

Women of Faith, Inc. is a ministry division of Thomas Nelson, Inc.

* Dates and locations subject to change.